MW00424440

FROM DECISION TO CLOSE

A 40-Step No Nonsense, Straight to the Point Guide to Buying a Home

SCOTTIE SMITH, II

ISBN-13: 978-1519419095
ISBN-10: 1519419090

Dedication

This book is dedicated to my Pops and Mom, Walter and Tammy Moten.

Thank you for always encouraging me to reach for the stars.

To my beautiful children Julian and Laila, my true reason for continuing to work so hard!

Also, my siblings. All 12 of you guys.

Katrina, Fred, Shawn, MAJOR. Whitney, Walter, Alethia, Joshua, Titus, Tamika, Ian, and Taryn. I love you all!

This first book is dedicated to you. The loves and encouragers of my life!

Contents

Acknowledgments

To my close friends and family that continually pushed me to complete this book, I thank you! Without you and your encouragement, this wouldn't have been possible.

And to the ones who were patient with me during my "off the grid" weekends. Thank you! Your patience, encouragement and understanding really helped me to follow through on my personal promises to myself!

So, You Want to Buy a Home?

Before you begin reading, I want you to ask yourself these questions. Do you know what you're about to get yourself into? Do you understand the realities of homeownership and what it means once you're considered a homeowner? I guess the real question should be, do you really WANT to know those things?

My goal has and will always be very simple, to help people! My vision for this book is for it to be the number one resource in America for people who are looking to become a homeowner, and more so, an educated and informed homeowner.

Back in 2007/2008, our economy went through a major financial turning point called, THE GREAT RECESSION! And many economists will tell you that the collapse of the housing market was one of the major factors and contributors to this Great Recession. I'm not an economist, but I've spent over 10 years working, researching and reviewing the real estate trends and markets and I agree.

The housing market was, in my opinion, the most influential part of the entire Great Recession.

I've sat on many panels throughout the years and have made the argument many times that the reason the housing market went belly-up is because of two reasons.

1. Uninformed, Misinformed or Uneducated Buyers

2. Predatory Lending Practices

Uninformed, misinformed or uneducated buyers went into the home buying process extremely green and often were taken advantage of by lenders and real estate professionals who were only looking out for themselves and their pocketbooks.

When I first started working in real estate I immediately recognized how easy it was to obtain a home loan. I actually witnessed it firsthand in 2007, when I was only 19 years old. This is when I purchased my first home. For the loan, I used my part time job as a bank teller where I was making less than forty thousand dollars per year and my financial aid and scholarship funds as proof of my down payment.

I got with who I thought was a great real estate agent, and went searching. No information, outside of my own knowledge, was provided to me and no expectations were set.

I met with the lender referred to me by my agent and 30 days after I submitted my offer, I was signing loan documents at the closing table. I was a college student, 19 years old, unable to consume alcohol (legally), but was now a homeowner.

That purchase worked out for me, but a day didn't pass without me thinking about how easy it was for me to get that home loan. So much so, that before the end of 2007, I purchased and sold two more investment properties. I really didn't understand how this was even possible.

But as the clock struck midnight and the calendars turned to 2008, things changed. FAST! Lenders weren't lending, houses weren't selling, and more and more displaced families came on my radar.

It wasn't until a year later that it dawned on me. As we approached the bottom of the real estate market, I noticed all of the foreclosures that were available nationwide. Homes were snatched from people who had committed to loans with adjustable interest rates. Most of these homeowners couldn't refinance their home's mortgage because the value was not there! The value of their home had dropped much lower than the purchase price so much so that the amount of the loan balance was much more than the value of the property. This should NEVER happen in real estate.

But it did.

And the reason for this is because in 2005, 2006 and 2007, if you didn't have the funds for your down payment, closing cost or any other fees, that was ok! Your lender would simply wrap those amounts into your loan. Sometimes up to 120% of the value of your home!

So what does that mean?

Let's look at it from this perspective. If you purchased a home using an FHA loan product (we'll dive deeper into what that is later in the book), your down payment (or equity position) is 3.5% of the home price. So on a $100,000 home that amount is $3,500. You must also consider your closing cost of about 3%. So we'll say an additional $3,000 was needed for closing costs. In total, you'd need $106,500 to purchase that home.

What should happen, and what happens now that the market has corrected, is the amount of your loan would be $96,500. You'd have that $3,500 equity in your home once you walk into your new front door -which is how things should be.

However, in the early 2000s, lenders would wrap both the down payment and closing cost into your initial home loan. So instead of having equity and having a lower loan balance than what the property is worth, homeowners had negative equity of $6,500 (down payment + the closing cost) in the home. It was like having a depreciated asset from the very moment of purchase, similar to a car.

This created a problem. When those adjustable rates increased, the home owners were exposed. The owners could no longer afford the home because the high interest rates increased their mortgage payment, and the likelihood of them being able to refinance to a lower rate was slim simply because the value was not there.

Predatory lenders played a dangerous role in this entire thing. Information was not often provided to the homebuyers about the consequences of this practice, and in my personal experience, it was never even discussed.

If a buyer knew the consequences of what they were doing, or were informed about what could go wrong, things would have turned out differently.

Why am I telling you this?

That answer is simple. I want you, the reader; the future homebuyer to understand all the negatives that are associated with not being an informed buyer. Understand that everything that glitters isn't gold and every opportunity that is presented to you is not the best thing.

I recommend that you speak with professionals and also research a little on your own before you jump into the home buying process. This book is a great place to start. You'll read multiple times throughout the book that a house and any piece of real estate is most people's largest investment. This will be the largest financial transaction that many people will ever make! So it's important that you're careful and aware of every part of the process.

Before you start working towards purchasing a home, do your due diligence and prepare as much as you can.

An informed and prepared buyer is someone who understands the process and who also understands what it means to be a homeowner. The responsibilities that come with this are huge.

Be sure that you are not another consumer that is taken advantage of by lenders and pure ignorance. If at any point during this period you hear a lender tell you that they can wrap any of the expenses into your loan, you RUN - fast and far.

Take advantage of the things you learn in this book and put them into action. Things learned aren't worth much if you aren't putting them into motion.

Over the next few months, consider these things and really think about what they mean. There is a workbook included with this book so that you can work through some of the things you may come across in this book. Feel free to share these with your family and even ask your hired professional to work through them with you.

We'll walk you through everything you need to know to be considered an informed buyer; from the initial decision to closing.

You'll be equipped with all the tools needed to make the right financial decision for you and your family! Let's jump into it!

Let's jump into it!

The Decision

The decision to purchase a home is one of the largest investment decisions that most people will make in their entire lives. It's really a big deal and because of this, there are many moving parts during the process that can, quite literally, drive a person insane. However, with proper planning and intentional action items, you can drastically reduce the difficulties of this process.

Deciding that you want to be a homeowner is the first step. Just like with any other goal, simply declaring what you want is the very start to the magic of becoming a homeowner. But let's think about what all should go into this decision. Over the next few weeks, consider the items in this chapter as you think about the possibilities of buying a home.

1. Do an analysis of your current living expenses

The decision to become a homeowner is a big one. And for most people the question "can I afford to purchase?" will inevitably come to mind. But what I encourage you to do is complete an analysis of your current living expenses. Think about the amount of money you are paying to live in the home, apartment, basement or room where you currently reside. Add in the lights, water, gas, cable and any other expenses you pay monthly. The number that you get is your current living expense (Disclaimer: if this amount is $0, think about staying where you are. You've got the perfect set-up and I'd hate for you to ruin a good thing!).

Now, according to the US Census Bureau, 25% of renters spend more than 50% of their monthly income on living expenses compared to homeowners who spend right around 35% of their income. If aft er you complete your analysis and you realize that you fall within that first bucket, then this book is especially for you. Not only as a guide to purchasing a home, but also as a guide to help you save more money every month. We'll go into budgeting more in detail in the next chapter, but during this week, you will definitely want to consider and possibly revamp your budget. If your income to living expense analysis gives you an amount higher than 35%, deciding to purchase a home isn't a bad financial decision for you.

2. Compare rent vs. buy

The age old questions surrounding homeownership that I continue to hear are, "Is it cheaper to rent or buy?" and "Will it cost me more to buy a home than to rent one?" and my answer is always a resounding, "IT DEPENDS."

If you only consider what you are actually paying every single month as the determining factors for the basis of your answer, then yes, sometimes it is cheaper to rent than to buy. However, there are a number of different key factors that one must take into account to get the true answer to that question.

Of course you want to consider the actual monthly payments, but you also want to consider a few other things such as the tax benefits of owning a home, equity building that is tied directly to your wealth, appreciation of the home's value, and resale value. When you consider all of the factors, it's actually more costly to NOT purchase than to continue renting. When you compare all of the benefits of homeownership and the cost savings associated with it to renting, you'll see that owning a home is the way to go.

3. Consider your first home as an investment

Listen people! This is your first home. And statistically speaking, it won't be your last! So take this opportunity to think about your home purchase as an investment. The theory that I normally teach my clients is the "Anything Theory," which states that *you can change anything about a house, except its location*. So stop and think about that for a second.

I understand it's easy to direct your attention to a home that already comes with the bells and whistles but that home typically comes at a premium. But, if you find a home that needs just a few repairs or upgrades you may have an opportunity to add value.

Channel your inner interior designer and make the property your own, all while saving on the purchase price. Think about the equity that you can build in a home by thinking like the thousands of investors around the country. So consider this approach as a viable option for you as you start to think through your decision of buying.

4. Prepare mentally for the process

I mentioned it before, but I'm going to mention it one more time. The home buying process is easily one of the most stressful processes that people go through. There are so many moving parts that it can drive you crazy. So it's great idea to prepare yourself.

It's not uncommon during the home buying process to experience all of the emotions that are humanly possible. Excitement, anger, joy, humiliation, frustration, anxiety, aggression, happiness, sadness and then all of those yet again. It can get ugly, people! But the trick to it all, is preparing yourself for it. Once you understand that things happen, there's really not much that can affect you negatively.

Understand that there are things that you cannot control and other things that you can. Keep a cool head and let the professionals that you will hire handle all of the mess! Besides, most of the emotions that come with the home buying process only appear because the buyers are unprepared for it. But that won't be you because you're reading this book! And once you complete it, you'll be 95% prepared for the process.

Buying a home can be a ton of work, but preparation is key, both financially and most importantly, mentally. Your mindset is an integral part of the plan, so be prepared.

There's a quote I read from H.L. Hunt that I really love: *"Decide what you want, decide what you are willing to exchange for it. Es-*

tablish your priorities and go to work." When you decide that home-ownership is your goal, there are a different set of priorities that come with that decision. You have to understand that this decision can actually change the trajectory of your financial future and requires that you adapt and change your current way of thinking. All for the greater good of owning a home!

The steps offered here are a great starting point for your decision making and, in my opinion, are some of the most important. Make the decision, write down the goal and then start to plan. It's as simple as that.

Get Your Financial House in Order

One of the single most important steps in preparing to purchase your home is getting your financial house in order. Many real estate professionals and mortgage lenders will tell you to be sure to speak with a lender before you even think about looking for a home. In fact, I've known many real estate agents to not even meet with a client without them having spoken with a mortgage lender. But what many people are not aware of, are the things that you should have in place before you consider speaking with a lender. This chapter covers a few of those things. Let's get our financial house in order! Over the next 6-8 weeks, consider putting these things into action to bring you that much closer to purchasing your home.

5. Find out what's on your credit report

Knowing what's on your credit report is a great place to start. It allows you to see what is being reported by your creditors and shows any new creditors your ability to pay your current obligations. Before you consider making any purchase that requires a loan of any sort, you should check into this. The three major bureaus, Transunion, Equifax and Experian are required to provide you a free copy of your reports once every 12 months. Take advantage of this by going to annual-creditreport.com. Please note that your credit reports are provided free but normally there is a separate charge to access your scores. Once you pull your reports, review them for accuracy. Be sure that everything on the report is yours. If there are any inaccuracies, reach out to the credit bureaus to make any disputes necessary. You want your credit reports to be clean once it's time to speak with a mortgage lender.

6. Find out your credit scores

One of the most common misconceptions about getting a home loan is that you need to have 700+ credit score to qualify. That is not always the case. Most lenders look for at least a 640 credit score. And some lending programs will allow for you to go down as low as 580. These products typically come with more aggressive interest rates, so my recommendation is that you shoot for 640 or higher. Once you have a decent hold on your credit score, it will be much easier for you to shop around for different loan products.

7. Be sure that you have a job

This should go without saying. If you want to qualify for a home loan, you must be an employed individual. If you are a W-2 employee, most lenders look for at least two years of stable employment. If you have recently switched employers, in most cases, they want to see that you are at least working in the same industry. This will be verified at some point in the lending process. An exception to this rule is if you are a recent college graduate that has been newly hired. The lender will usually count the years that you were in school as "employment" if your current position is in the area of interest that you studied while in school. Most lenders will require you provide a school transcript with proof of graduation and major.

If you are a self-employed or 1099 individual, this rule somewhat differs for you. Lenders that do work with self-employed individuals require that you provide at least two years of tax returns. From there they will calculate your monthly income by adding both year's adjusted gross income and then dividing by 24 months. This simple calculation will give the lender a basis for what you can afford to pay monthly. In each case, be it self-employment or W-2 employment, you will need to show a stable work history of at least two years. So, if you don't have a job currently, start looking!

8. Make a commitment to start saving money for a down payment, closing costs and reserves

The home buying process has its fair share of surprises that you should be financially prepared for. Outside of your normal down payment and closing cost requirements, there are other expenses that a potential homeowner must be prepared to pay out of pocket.

Things such as earnest money, home inspection, home appraisal and other lender required fees, will come up during the process.

If your plan is to become a homeowner, making a commitment to start saving NOW is not just important, it's imperative to a successful home buying experience. The biggest expense that you should save for is your down payment. That number can be as low as 3% or as high as 20% depending on your specific loan criteria, loan program and the state that you want to live in. The Federal Housing Admin-istration (FHA) typically has loan products that require a down pay-ment of as little as 3.5% for most buyers. There are specific require-ments for these programs and I recommend discussing them with your lender when that time comes.

The second largest expense you'll need to save for is closing costs. In some cases (depending on the current market) the seller may be willing to provide concessions for closing costs. But it is safe to save between 3% and 6% of the price of the home just to be completely covered. There are a number of down payment assistance grant pro-grams available for most first time home buyers, and I always recom-mend looking into those. But, if there is one thing that I've learned in my short ten years in the industry is that you should always CYA (Cover Your Assets). So save, save, save!

9. Pay every bill on time

This is essential to keeping a solid credit profile and score. Paying all of your bills on time not only helps builds your credit scores, but also shows your potential mortgage lender that you are capable of managing debt properly. Your credit report and profile are the key indicators for mortgage approval. Unless you are purchasing a home with all cash, your credit is crucial to the entire process and just one missed payment can drastically reduce the likelihood of you being approved for your loan. So be sure that you are paying every bill on time! Automate your payments to make this easy for you.

10. Intentional deposits into and withdrawals out of your accounts

At first read, this may seem a little weird. But it's extremely important! And here's why. When your mortgage application and all of the supporting documents are submitted to the mortgage underwriter, they will review and scrutinize every single thing in the file; including your bank accounts and statements. In most cases, the underwriter will look for deposit amounts that match your payroll check. Any deposit outside of your normal job payroll check will raise a red flag and will require a detailed explanation letter as to where this deposit came from.

Lenders do this to ensure that the funds you are claiming in your bank accounts as legal assets have not come from an illegal source. If there have been any large deposits from family or friend accounts, the underwriter will ask for additional supporting documentation from that person's accounts. With the rise of money laundering and illegal transactions, underwriters have taken a serious stance on this. If the deposits can't be explained, the underwriter won't count those funds towards your mortgage approval and, in some cases, it can negatively affect your final approval.

You want to be intentional with these deposits and even consider having separate household accounts for your normal payroll deposit and for all other things. If you haven't already started doing this, it's ok. The underwriter will only look at your past three month's statements. In extreme cases, they will go back six months. So act and plan accordingly. In short, be sure that you are able to explain in detail every deposit that comes into your account that is not from your normal paycheck. Check out the household accounts diagram included in the workbook and consider using this as a financial road-map for your household deposits and withdrawals.

11. Budget, budget, budget

Budgeting is the foundation for every home and business in the WORLD. It's important that you realize as a soon to be homeowner that if you haven't already created a budget, then NOW is the perfect time for you to start. Detailing your financial affairs out so that you can see them all in one place, helps for you to prepare yourself for the fi nancial responsibility that comes with owning a home. This is a key element in the entire process and once you get into the habit of budgeting, it's easier for you to manage debt, save and even invest in other things. We've included a budgeting worksheet for you to con-sider using. Check that out in the Appendix of this book.

12. Have a conversation with a mortgage lender to learn how much home you can afford

Now that you've gotten a stronghold on your finances, you should have a conversation with a lender to determine how much home you can afford. Your lender will review your credit report, credit score, financial assets and then determine your debt to income ratio. From this simple equation, your lender will let you know the maximum loan amount that you can qualify for. From there, in most cases, they will issue you a pre-qualification or pre-approval letter, which is your golden ticket to start your home search.

A pre-approval letter lets sellers know that you're a serious buyer and have done the due diligence needed to secure financing to purchase. That pre-approval letter gives you leverage when submitting offers on homes and allows for stronger negotiation. Do not start looking for homes until you have completed this step.

Getting your financial house in order is no easy task but it is completely manageable. By following the steps outlined here, you'll be that much closer to becoming a homeowner. Be detailed in your approach and intentional in your strategy. Preparing to purchase a home can be done very easily if you put the time and effort into getting your financial house in order.

Find Your Home

13. Hire a real estate agent or REALTOR®

Ok, I get it! We live in a world that allows for us to access millions of bits of information at the push of a button. The internet...so useful, but yet so harmful. It's simple for many people to believe they can trust their own learned knowledge of real estate to navigate the home buying process, however, there is nothing that can substitute the hundreds of hours of classroom training, licensing, education and experience that a real estate agent possesses. Attempting to navigate the rough waters of a real estate transaction without the help of a real estate agent is quite similar to walking into a courtroom without an attorney. Can you do it? SURE...But should you? Absolutely not.

As a homebuyer, you want to be sure that you have the right person in your corner protecting you every step of the way. Someone who will negotiate on your behalf and fight for the things you want. This is what a real estate agent is hired to do. And as a buyer, a real estate agent will work on your behalf, FREE OF CHARGE! You read that right. As a buyer, you are typically not responsible for paying the agent for their work. Of course this varies state by state, but here in Texas, the buyer's agent's commission is paid by the seller's broker. You can always do an online search for local real estate agents in your area and find one that works best for you. It's best, however, that you search for a REALTOR®. The common misconception is that a REALTOR® and a licensed real estate agent are the same. However, this is not true. A REALTOR® is actually a real estate agent who has taken the oath and accepted the standards of the National Association of REALTORS®. To keep things simple; they are held to much higher ethical and legal standards than those who have not taken this oath. In short, if you are purchasing a home, it's imperative that you hire a REALTOR®. Be sure to ask around for real estate agent referrals and verify that they are REALTORS®. Friends and family are typically more than willing to pass along that information to you.

14. Understand the local market

Buyer's Market vs. Seller's Market

Once you identify your REALTOR®, be sure that you meet in person to discuss the current market. The key to a successful transaction is knowledge and information. The more you know, the easier it will be to navigate things. You and your REALTOR® should have a conversation about the difference between a buyer's market and a seller's market and how to proceed in each case. Never trust the national media but be sure to listen to the local experts. For instance, at the time of the writing of this book (August 2015), here in Texas it is a seller's market. This is also true for most areas in the United States. However, in the St. Louis, Missouri market, it's currently a buyer's market. As a buyer you want to know the difference between the two because it will let you know how to proceed.

Let's put things into perspective here. The type of market that any area is in all depends on one word; INVENTORY. Inventory, in the real estate world, means the number of homes that are currently on the market and available for sale. Most real estate professionals will determine what type of market their area is in based on the number of months' worth of inventory that are available for sale. A balanced market is right at six month's inventory; which means that if from that point on, there were no additional homes listed on the market for sale, then all of the homes currently available would be sold in six months. Anything over six months is a buyer's market, which means that there are plenty of homes available for buyers. Anything less than six months is considered a seller's market, which means that there are not very many homes available. Depending on the type of market your area is considered to be in (buyer's vs. seller's), your search and offer strategy will vary. Your REALTOR® should initiate this conversation, but if they don't, be sure to ASK! This is very important.

15. Communicate your search criteria

Now that you've hired your REALTOR® and you have a thorough understanding of the market, it's now time to communicate to them your home search criteria. Think about the things that you want in your home. How many bedrooms? How many bathrooms? How big of a home do you want. Two-story or one-story? Condo or townhome? Think long and hard about these things, and about everything that you want in your home. It's so important to consider these and to be able to communicate clearly to your REALTOR® so that you're able to maximize your time with them. Be sure to be as specific and detailed as possible. The last thing you'd want to do is have your REALTOR® send things to you that don't come close to what you want in your home. And remember the sky is the limit here and it's really all about your budget. But keep in mind the "Anything Theory"- *you can change anything about home except its location.*

Set the criteria so you can set the pace of what you'll view with your REALTOR®.

16. View homes online via your agent's MLS

The multiple listing service (or MLS) is a database of currently listed and available homes in your market area. Most REALTORS® will have access to this database and can share listings with you that meet your criteria. It is the most up-to-date and accurate information available, as its input is directly from the REALTORS® who are selling and helping clients buy homes.

Most agents will take your criteria and do a specified search in the MLS for exactly what you want. Considering the location, square footage, number of bedrooms and bathrooms that you indicated to them, they'll find exactly what you're looking for...sometimes. I bring the MLS and its accuracy into the conversation because REALTORS® have proprietary information that only they have access to. Sites such as Trulia.com, Zillow.com and Homes.com often have inaccurate information. They even go so far as to explain how inaccurate they are in their website disclaimers.

To make your home search as stress-free as possible, trust your REALTOR® to find exactly what's on the market. If you would like to search independently, I recommend using realtor.com or any of your local agent's websites. Do not, and I repeat do not, use Trulia or Zillow.

In my experience, a client will send over an address that is listed on these sites, and the home was sold months ago. In the Texas market, the two sites don't have access to the sold prices or dates. I say this because I want to save you the frustration that comes with seeing a house online that excites you, but then fi nding out the information posted is wrong! Tread lightly. Use your local REALTOR'S® resources or realtor.com to search for homes online. You'll thank me later!

17. Narrow down your selection to your top picks

After a few days of shuffling through the homes that your REALTOR® has sent you electronically, it's now time to select and narrow down your top picks. It's not uncommon for you to want to see every single home that's listed, that's really just the excitement! But depending on the market that you're in, you may not have that luxury. If it is a seller's market, for instance, it'll be extremely important for you to be strategic in the homes you select as favorites because homes typically sell much quicker. You'll maximize your time with your REALTOR® by narrowing down your search to your top choices. Now typically, I recommend choosing the top four or five homes that you absolutely love but again, it all depends on the market and how fast the homes are selling in your area. That number can fluctuate up or down. Remember that communication is key. If you communicate to your real estate agent just what you want in your home, your list should be filled with homes that you will love. Take a little bit of time and slim down that list.

18. Schedule time to view your selected homes

After you've selected your top picks, it's now time to go and view them. During this time, you and your REALTOR® will need to coordinate your schedules in order to view the homes in a reasonable amount of time. What many people don't know is that a REALTOR® is needed to go and view the home. REALTORS® have access to showing services that allow them to schedule viewings with their clients and notify the sellers that they are trying to do so. Although you may want to just jump up and go, it really doesn't work like that. Be sure that your real estate professional has scheduled all of the home viewings well in advance so that there are no last minute issues. Have them send confirmation to you just to verify. When you take a tour of the home, be sure to thoroughly examine it. Here are a few questions you should keep in mind:

- Are the rooms large enough?
- What is the distance from work, school, entertainment or places of worship?
- How is the neighborhood?

- Are the closets large enough for my clothes? - Is the kitchen functional?

- Can I see myself living in this house?

The greatest suggestion I can give a home buyer is, DO NOT IMPULSE SHOP. Unlike clothes, shoes and accessories, there is no 30 day return policy on a house. If you purchase it, you are stuck with it until it's time to sell. So spend a little time in each home and select the one that is right for you!

19. Make an offer

You've found it! The perfect home! You've asked all the questions listed above about this home and all the answers check out. You want this home as your own! When you've gotten to this point, it's now time to make an offer. Your REALTOR® should offer their insight and expertise once this time comes, but keep in mind that time is of the essence. If you love a home, make the offer. No need to wait or drag out the process. Your REALTOR®'s job is to negotiate the best deal for you considering the current market and your job is to trust that they will. When making an offer though, there are a few things that you must keep in mind.

An offer is much more than just the offer price. The offer price is just one piece of the puzzle letting the seller know how much you are willing to pay for the home. But also consider the following:

1. Seller's contribution to your closing cost, title policy, and home warranty expense

2. Number of days until closing

3. Inspection period

4. Financing conditions (if you are using a loan)

An offer is typically in writing and is usually prepared by your RE-ALTOR® on contract forms. Your offer to purchase the home is not a guarantee that the home is yours. It's simply a notification to the seller of the terms that you are willing to abide by in order to purchase the home. Once you've made the offer, the seller can do one of three things. They can reject the offer, accept the offer or counter the offer. Reject and accept are pretty self-explanatory, however, if a seller counters your offer this means that they may accept some parts of the offer but reject other parts. They will tell you, usually in writing, their terms that they accept and/or reject.

Receiving a counteroffer is not a bad thing. It's a great thing and it lets you know that they are willing to negotiate with you in order to make the sale. You won't go at this alone. Your REALTOR® will walk you through this process. Once you and the sellers have come to a complete agreement of terms, the offer is signed and executed. You now have your dream home under contract! Get excited! Because you're one step closer to becoming a homeowner. But the real work is about to start.

Prepare for Closing

You've prepared for this day. You've planned, saved and considered all options. You've done the due diligence. And finally, you have the perfect home under contract. Now what? From this point forward, you'll need to go into overdrive. This is when everything pays off; all the hard work and painful weeks of planning. They come full circle! You've made it to this point and now it's time for you to prepare for closing.

Over the next few weeks, you'll be required to prepare and plan further. Fight through it, because you're nearing the final steps of the home buying process; the closing! The closing is the end of the transaction process where both the seller and the buyer go to sign all of the legal documents needed to transfer ownership from one party to the other. This is typically done by a closing agent or title company. Getting to the closing table can take time, but you've worked hard to get to this point, so you should be ok! Consider these items on your way to the closing table.

20. Submit contract to the title company

With the contract in hand and a smile on your face, your next steps should be towards the title company. In most states, the title company and escrow officers will research the title on the property. A title company ensures that the title of any piece of property is legitimate and then provides title insurance for it. Title insurance is an insurance policy designed to protect owners and lenders against loss or damage due to title defects. Title insurance provides peace of mind as well as protection for any damages a property owner incurs as a result of unforeseen legal issues involving ownership in the property.

Your REALTOR® will deliver the fully executed contract and earnest money to the title company so that they may start preparation for the closing. The earnest money is the money put down by you, the buyer, to serve as damages in the event that you default on the contract. There is no set amount for this and different markets have different norms as to how much a buyer should offer. But note, this amount is refunded back at closing and is applied to the overall costs to the buyer.

The title company will research the chain of title and deed and check to see if there are any liens on the property. If there are issues with any of these items, all parties will be notifi ed. The seller's responsibility is to deliver the property to the new owner with a clear title. It's the title company's job to ensure that this happens. A home buyer should never move forward with the purchase of a home without a clear title!

21. Get a home inspection

In any real estate contract, it is my firm belief that there should be an option period included. An option period is a specific time frame, usually included in the contract that would allow for you, the buyer, to terminate the contract for any reason. It gives the buyer the right to cancel or end the contract within a specific number of days, for a price agreed upon by all parties. This option period allows the buyer a certain amount of time to have an inspection done on the property thus protecting them from the potential hazards of buying a home that is a "lemon." The length of the option period is part of the negotiated terms of the contract, but I've typically seen between five to ten days for this. During this period, find a reputable home inspector in your area and hire them. A home inspector will tell you everything about the home you have under contract. Everything from the top of the roof to the bottom of the foundation, and everything else in between.

This inspection is not a pass or fail, but rather a detailed look at the inner workings of the home you are about to purchase. Although an inspection isn't required, I always suggest that a buyer have one done. Your home inspector should provide you with a detailed report of the inspection. Review this in detail and use it as a renegotiation tool.

If there are items in the report that require seller attention, provide an amendment to the contract and request the seller to address those items. You'll want to ensure that the home is in livable condition before ownership transfers. With this in mind, please note that many pre-existing homes will have adverse issues on the inspection report. My general rule of thumb, and (of course this depends on the market) if it does not affect the structure, foundation, electrical, plumbing or roofing of the home, it isn't that big of a deal. Not to say that you shouldn't request the seller to address any of the other things, but anything outside of those six, it shouldn't be a major deal killer. But nevertheless, as a savvy home buyer, please remember; *"For Your Protection, Get an Inspection."*

22. Submit final paperwork to your lender

You're almost there! The finish line is near. But, the last hurdle includes getting your loan finalized from your mortgage lender. Although you've done all you could in the very beginning of the process, the lenders are going to still ask a few more questions. The most important thing to remember here is the "2..2..2 and 2 rule." This rule sets out exactly what you should have fully prepared for your lender and their underwriters at this point in the process. Two years of your W-2's, two years of tax returns, two months' worth of bank statements and two months' worth of paycheck stubs. The mortgage underwriters are going to require all of these documents to verify income and proof of job stability. Understand that any mortgage lender that approves you for a home loan is taking a major financial risk by lending that money to you. They will do everything to confirm that you can handle the responsibility of that debt. They will invade all of your financial privacy and become one with your financial affairs. That is the cost of borrowing from mortgage lenders. It's normal to feel like they are invading your privacy, especially because they really are. They will scrutinize in great detail everything about your financials, but by taking the steps detailed in the "Getting Your Financial House in Order" chapter, you should be fine. The lender may ask for explanations about certain things that you provided, so preparing yourself for this ahead of time will help you to decrease stress. Once you send the "2..2..2 and 2" over to your lender, finalizing your loan should be a breeze.

23. Order and review home appraisal

Once you've received the executed contract and completed and approved the inspection, have your lender order the appraisal. This part is fun, but can cause a bit of anxiety in the process. The appraisal is the valuation of a home done by a licensed and certified board appraiser. The appraiser's job is to place a true value of the property based on information that is presented in the market. Their job is also to ensure that the banks are not lending more money on the property than it's worth. They are there to protect the banks, so conservatism typically plays a large role.

If your home's appraisal value comes back lower than the amount of the contracted price, most lenders will not lend unless the difference is either made up in cash by the buyer, or the price of the contract is amended to match the price of the appraisal. Unless you are purchasing with all cash, you will surely have to go through the appraisal process. Don't let it get you down, but be patient.

24. Understand your payments

So listen. I'll be blunt with you! What most online mortgage sites show you as an estimate of your monthly payment is usually incomplete.

I've had clients come to my office and tell me on many occasions that they believe they can afford a half a million dollar home because the internet told them their mortgage would only be $2,200. Listen people! The internet only tells you what you want to know. Not what you need to know. What you need to know and understand is that your complete mortgage payment includes a few different components.

Typically, what you see posted online are principal and interest. But, what they forget to tell you about is the taxes, insurance and primary mortgage insurance. Your taxes and insurance all depend on the city, state or other municipality you are purchasing in. Your insurance depends on the company that you select. Combine the two with primary mortgage insurance, and this gives you your full monthly payment. Now, there are some exceptions to this rule, namely if your mortgage loan does not have primary mortgage insurance. If this is the case your monthly payment will be cheaper. Having an in depth conversation with your lender about this isn't a bad idea. They should be provide you an estimate of your monthly payment, including all components, prior to closing. Understand this early on in the process so that there are no surprises in the end. This preparedness creates responsible homeowners; and you definitely want to be responsible!

25. Estimate and consider your closing costs

Earlier in this book, we discussed in great detail the importance of budgeting and saving for your down payment and closing costs. We stressed the importance of that to prepare you for this very moment.

During this part of the process, you should work closely with your lender to fully understand and estimate how much money you'll need to bring to the closing table. Your closing costs are the fees paid at closing. Typically these costs include fees from your lender, the title company, or closing agent, any attorneys involved, as well as possible REALTOR® related charges. Your closing costs are separate from your down payment and should be budgeted differently. Although you will bring one check or money order to closing, these two expenses should be considered separately. A simple conversation with your lender will help you understand the amount of your closing cost. Be sure to estimate these before the big closing date so there are no surprises.

26. Complete final loan processing and underwriting

If you followed the steps in the "Getting Your Financial House in Order" chapter, this process should be relatively fluid. Simply submit all of the final documents to the underwriter and wait for the final "Clear to Close." Those three words will be like music to your ears. After you've gone through the ringer, spilled your guts outs and made yourself financially vulnerable, you'll be jumping for joy to hear those beloved three words. "Clear to Close" means your loan application and file have received the final stamp of approval and will soon be funded. You'll need to review the final HUD, complete a final walk-through of your home and then get to the title company to sign your papers.

27. Select/purchase a home warranty

So, this term may be new to some people, but it's a life saver for a new home owner. A home warranty, is a contract between a homeowner and a home warranty company that provides repairs and replacement services on a home's major components, such as AC systems, plumbing, appliances, pools and many other items. It acts as insurance for the things your normal insurance company does not protect. I'm sure you're wanting to know why this is important and why you should get one. Well, listen up! You want to trust me on this one. If you are purchasing a pre-existing or pre-owned home, the likelihood of things breaking down within the first year of ownership is much higher than if you were purchasing a newly constructed home. So, you want to have protection against these malfunctions or breakdowns, because sometimes the cost can be unbearable. Most home warranties will protect you and your family from the financial burden that comes with unexpected breakdown of appliances, AC units, and hot water heaters. Depending on the plan that you purchase from the home warranty company, you may even be able to get ancillary services such as, free rekeying, new thermostat installation as well as other things. Be sure that you research your home warranty company to ensure that they are licensed and authorized to operate in the state that you live in. Home warranties, in my opinion, will be your BEST FRIEND! They can run from $200 to $600, depending on the company. Sometimes you can even ask for the seller to pay for this! Test out your negotiating skills and just ask! Remember these two words. HOME WARRANTY. You'll thank me later.

28. Get clear to close from lender

Now listen here. You've waited long enough. You've prepared and completed everything the lender has asked of you. And up to this point you've done nothing but wait. Then one day, via email, fax or maybe even text, you get the three magic words from your lender that state, we are CLEAR TO CLOSE! At this moment, you can start to jump for joy and celebrate your victory. These are by far the three greatest words that a mortgage borrower will hear during the entire process. This is the final piece to the puzzle. Once you have this, your lender will send closing instructions to the title company. From there, the title company will put together all of the documents necessary to close on your home. Included in these documents will be all of your lender required forms, your deed as well as a final summary of all of the expenses and fees required. This summary is your HUD 1 settlement statement. You'll have an opportunity to review this before your closing date.

29. Review the final HUD 1 settlement statement

A couple days before closing, the title company should provide you with what is called the HUD 1settlement statement. This statement includes a detailed outline of all your expenses for the home. It separates the buyer and seller's expenses and allows you to see line by line for all the things you're charged for at closing. The last number you will see at the end of your HUD 1 summary is your "cash to close," which is the amount of money you need to bring on the day of closing.

It's important as a new buyer to review this statement in great detail before you sign and approve it. Once you get to the closing table, it's difficult to change this. What you want to do is review the entire document for any mistakes, clear errors, name changes, address changes and things of the sort. You want to ensure that you pay close attention to title fees, lender fees and estimates provided by your loan officer. Your lender will also review this document to ensure that all of the information is correct.

Be sure to pay close attention to the amount of the insurance and the prorated taxes that are on the HUD1settlement statement. If there are mistakes, it's okay. You'll be able to recommend changes prior to closing. Review - review - review. Once this is done, you're that almost there. It's time to go and get your house.

30. Complete a final walkthrough

Your final walkthrough of your home is the final step before heading over to the title company to sign documents. We've gotten the final clear to close, you've reviewed the final HUD and now it's time to take a final tour through your home. The mission is simple! To make sure that the place is in the exact same condition (or better) that it was in when you initially made your offer! Also, you want to be sure to re-inspect any items that you requested the seller address prior to closing. Trust, but verify!

If there are any items that seem out of place, be sure to discuss with the seller prior to signing any documents. Have them complete everything that is not done or is out of place before you take possession of the home. Always remember to do this before you sign because your signature is an indication that you're accepting the home in its current state. Remember to CYA! Inspect, inspect, inspect! But ultimately, have fun with your final walkthrough; because the reality is...YOU'RE ABOUT TO BE A HOMEOWNER!!!!!

31. Gather items to bring to closing

There are certain items that a buyer must bring to the closing table in order to finalize the transaction. You want to make sure you have all of these items so that on the day of closing things go as smoothly as possible, with no surprises.

After you review the HUD 1 settlement statement, you should know the exact amount of money needed to fulfill your obligation at closing. That amount is considered your "cash to close" and is usually brought in the form of a cashier's check or money order made out to the title company. You should have a conversation with the title company beforehand about their requirements for this. In some cases, a title company will require a wire transfer of funds that are over a certain amount. You want to get this ahead of time so that there are no delays in your funding. It's recommended that this is handled two to three days before the day of closing.

In addition to your cash to close, you will need to bring a valid government issued photo ID. Usually a driver's license or state identification card will do the trick. Other forms of ID that a title company will accept are a government issued passport, and sometimes, a green card or visa, if you are purchasing with cash.

Having all of these items available prior to closing will help you to transition from the homebuyer to homeowner.

Reminder: Be sure to gather your documents the day before closing.

You've done it! You've worked through all of these steps and have finally gotten through the daunting task of closing on your new home. On your closing day, you'll sign what may seem like hundreds of documents but it will all be worth it. Be sure that you read over everything before you sign and be prepared! The key to a simplified home buying process is to prepare yourself as much as you can yet allowing for your real estate professional to help you get to the finish line. Closing typically brings a good amount of emotions, and goal is to ensure that you know about all the surprises before they come. The cheat sheet of home buying, per se! Enjoy the day that you close on your home and maintain a level head throughout the closing. If you followed these steps, then you're ready to go! Close on your home, collect the keys from the seller and start moving! Congratulations, today is YOUR DAY! You are now a living, breathing, and property tax paying homeowner! Create memories, share stories and collect love in your new home. Welcome to homeownership.

Home
Sweet Home

32. Get the keys from the previous owner

You've officially closed and funded on your home and now the home belongs to you. You'll need to coordinate with the seller so that you may get the keys. Although this may seem like a "duh" moment, many people forget about this step. Get with your agent so that you can pick up the keys to your home. I recommend that you contact your home warranty company to have them come out and either rekey the locks or change them out completely. This is a fairly simple process and shouldn't take much brain power to get it done.

33. Transfer or turn on all utilities to your new home

Usually this step can be done before you close, but if you're into saving a few dollars, I'd wait until after closing to have the utilities turned on. You will want to get in contact with the service providers that you plan to use prior to closing to schedule your service activation, but be sure to confirm with them post-closing. The last thing you want is a delayed move in because the electricity isn't working. And if you're like most new home buyers who purchase during the summer months, you'll surely need the air conditioner working while you bring in the boxes. Just remember, planning is key. Reach out to them ahead of time and you'll be just fine.

34. Have your new home professionally cleaned

Unless you're moving into a home that was newly built, I always recommend getting the home professionally cleaned by a maid service. Don't risk moving your furniture into a home that ultimately will need to be deep cleaned. Don't double work yourself. Schedule a cleaner to come out and handle that for you. I recommend using the Tidy-Clean App for this as it allows for you to select a few options for your cleaner.

35. Complete a change of address with the post ofice

Your move is important and there are a ton of moving parts, so it's easy to forget about this very essential part of the entire process; completing a change of address with the post office. If you receive mail where you are, all you would need to do is visit the U.S. Postal Service's website and complete an address change. It typically takes all of ten minutes to complete. If you don't, you could end up missing some very important piece of mail. Especially if the home has been vacant for a long period of time. Sometimes the mail carrier will continue to skip the mailbox at your home because they've gotten used to the home being vacant. So be sure to do this as soon as possible. Additionally, make sure you notify the title company at closing that your new home's address will be the delivery address for all of the closing documents. You don't want to just do an address change with the USPS, you always want to notify all of your creditors, banks and even your family members.

36. Prepare for the big move

Boxes, beds and dressers! Shoes, kitchenware and couches! Books, shelves, tables and chairs. It's moving day! If you want to save money, I recommend just renting a truck, gathering some friends and spending the day moving things on your own. But if you're anything like me, after packing, you may not want to do anything else. Find local and reliable movers that will safely transport your furniture to your new place. Just a few hints; be sure that they have a good rating with the Better Business Bureau or good reviews on Yelp. Also make sure the movers are bonded and/or insured. This protects you and your belongings from any potential damages. Lastly, if you value any of your furniture, I'd stay away from movers that advertise discount services on Craigslist.

37. Contact the homeowner's association

If you've purchased a home that is in a homeowner's association, I recommend getting in contact with that association to get as much information as possible. Ask about meetings, the budget and what your dues cover. Make the decision to be an active member of the HOA so that you can have a say it what goes on. Not all HOA's are created equally and although their job is to ensure that the homes in the neighborhood hold or increase their value, you want to be sure that they don't abuse their power. Do a little research on HOA's and what they can and can't do. Remember, they can work for you, or against you but it's up to you to be informed. Pick up the phone and make contact with them, immediately!

38. Meet the neighbors

Be friendly! Go meet the neighbors. You're in a new area with only a few friends. Take a stroll down the street and check out the neighborhood. Stop and talk to people that are outside, and spark up a conversation about different things to do. The people make the community and you should imbed yourself in it. Ask about the neighborhood and homeowner's associations. Ask about the best places to eat, run or hang out. If this is going to be your home, meet your new extended family.

39. File homestead tax exemptions

One of the major benefits you'll receive as a homeowner are the tax deductions for mortgage interest and property taxes paid. To that point, if your home is your primary residence, some states offer what is called a homestead exemption. A homestead exemption lowers your taxes by removing a portion of your home's value from taxation. To apply for this exemption, a homeowner must occupy the property as their homestead on January 1 of the tax year in which the exemption was applied. Which means, if you purchased your home aft er January 1, you will need to wait until the following year to apply for this exemptions. The forms are usually online and it is free to apply. Take advantage of this the very moment that you are able to. This will save you thousands of dollars over the years.

40. Throw the biggest housewarming party

You've earned it and you flat out deserve it. You've prepared for some time, you've saved and researched as much as any person can possibly do! You've spent the day moving or watching the movers handle your precious belongings. You've met the neighbors and had an in depth conversation with the HOA about why you can't paint the front door a bright green color. You've arranged things in their perfect place and organized as much as one could possibly do. Now let's have some fun. Throw a party! A housewarming! Take this opportunity to show off what you've worked so hard to get. Fire up the barbeque pit, pull out the punch bowl and kick back. This is always fun, and my favorite party...the gifts. In your invitation out to your friends and family, make sure they know that gifts are accepted! It's a fun way to receive gifts, show off your new place and finally enjoy your new home! Congratulations, you deserve it! You're now a homeowner and you should be proud. You've acquired your piece of the American dream!

Home Sweet Home!!

10 Commandments of Home Buying

1. Thou shalt NOT change jobs, become self-employed or quit your job during the home-buying process.

2. Thou shalt NOT buy a car, truck or van.

3. Thou shalt NOT use credit cards excessively or let current accounts fall behind.

4. Thou shalt NOT spend money you have set aside for closing.

5. Thou shalt NOT omit debts or liabilities from your loan application.

6. Thou shalt not buy furniture prior to closing.

7. Thou shalt not incur any new credit inquiries onto your credit report.

8. Thou shalt NOT make large deposits into your accounts without:

   a. Checking with your lender

   b. Being able to explain in detail the origins of that deposit.

9. Thou shalt NOT change bank accounts.

10. Thou shalt NOT co-sign a loan for anyone before closing.

The Reality

Becoming a homeowner is a major accomplishment and requires a great deal of work. But maintaining your home requires even more. It's a major responsibility that requires you, the homeowner, to be a good steward of your gift .

My mother once told me as a child growing up that "to whom much is given much is required," and that statement is so true for you, the new homeowner. You've been blessed with what could be one of your largest financial assets thus far, now it is your responsibility to maintain it.

Take care of your home with regular maintenance and lawn care. Make sure your home shines to the world! Be sure to take pride in your home, and show love to your neighborhood. And know this; you are responsible for the leaking toilet, the cracked window and the squeaky doors, not your landlord. I understand that making the transition from renter to homeowner can be tough and it does require a mindset shift, but the reality is, it can be done.

What you see in front of you is yours, not someone else's, so the commitment to being a good steward of what you have will be needed now more than ever. Be bold, be excited but be responsible for your house. Take the opportunity to enjoy it, entertain in it and create memories in it. Start a family, adopt a pet or even let a pass through traveler couch surf in your living room. Do it all! But whatever you do, be sure that you maintain your home both financially and physically.

Enjoy your new home and be sure to write or email me and let me know how your process went! I'm extremely happy that you've made it through this entire book and have implemented what you've learned into your home buying experience. My passion and drive stems from ensuring that people all over the country are well educated on the home buying process and well equipped with the tools needed to make informed decisions along the way. A well-educated buyer will inevitably become a well-educated homeowner, and that is what is important.

As a Thank You for Your Purchase,
We Would Like To Give You
Our Home Buyer's Workbook 100% Free!
Download the Free Workbook at
www.scottiesmith.co/FromD2C

Can you do me a favor?

Thank you for purchasing this book! I really appreciate all of your feedback, and I love hearing what you have to say.

I need your input to make the next version better.

Please leave me a helpful REVIEW on Amazon and tell the world how much you've learned!

Thanks so much!!

Scottie

About the Author

Scottie Smith, II started his real estate career at the age of 18. He bought and sold multiple properties before the legal drinking age of 21. As a licensed real estate professional in in Texas, he, along with his team of expert real estate advisors, has brokered millions of dollars in real estate sales helping people all across the country realize the dream of homeownership.

As the Broker and Owner of Scottie Smith, II & Associates Real Estate Advisor, Scottie has a simple goal; to help people. His lifelong mission has and will always be to help people, using his passion for real estate as the vehicle to do so.

Scottie's mission is to help as many people as possible to become homeowners because he truly believes that homeownership is the American Dream.